Lessons Learned from My Parents

Barbara Spencer Dunn

Highly Favored Publishing™
Bowie, Maryland

Highly Favored Publishing™
Bowie, Maryland 20716
www.highlyfavoredpublishing.com

This book is dedicated to my parents, Vernon Spencer
and Novella Spencer (born Erma Della Ball)

--January 6, 2007

God impressed upon my heart today that I had not done enough to share my testimony of the childhood I was blessed to have through the stewards God placed in charge of me, Vernon and Novella Spencer. My parents were truly a godsend, and I know that from the bottom of my heart. They were placed in my life to prepare me for the *Kingdom Assignment* that God personally created me to fulfill. My childhood was so rich! Although when I think about the money we had and the house we lived in, I realize now we would have been considered poor. However, we were so rich in the things of God that I never realized we were financially poor until I was in my 30s. Nevertheless, our house was truly a home.

****

Children become the recipients of all that God intended when their parents take the time to model obedience to God in their walk. As children, our purpose in life is guided by our individual understanding of the things we begin to embrace at an early age. When you have parents who believe in God and through that faith guide you according to His will, if you choose to be obedient to their guidance, you do not have to journey through a winding life path to get to the purpose intended for your life. This type of godly guidance is what I was blessed to receive from my loving, God-fearing parents. It was a guided path to my purpose.

The blessing of having parents who believe what God says in his Word, and also do what is in His Word, cannot be easily expressed. My parents loved my sisters, Frances Spencer Lark and Lillie (Mico) Spencer Scott, and me. Their love provided us with a childhood that was so rich we did not realize we were poor financially because our lives were so enriched by the things that were really important. Although our dad was a pastor of a church, outside of God and each other, we were our parents' priority. I learned so much from their daily walk and how they interacted with each other and with us girls. They set aside time to embrace each of us at our point of need, and they loved us in a way that caused us to love each other, as well. Everything they did showed a type of love that can only come from God. All of our friends loved them, as well, and our home was a place where everyone knew they were welcome. My mom and dad were ordinary people who took extraordinary steps to love like God loved and practice His command of obedience in everything they did. They modeled what they taught us in action more than in words. I cannot express how thankful to God I am to have had them as my parents.

I believe God's plan for my life included placing me in the loving stewardship of Vernon and Novella Spencer. Although they both left this earthly home and transitioned to their home in glory six months apart in 1991, after 51 ½ years of marriage, they are still very present in my heart and always will be. I love you, Mom and Dad, and will continue to share these wonderful lessons learned so other children will be granted an opportunity to experience loving parents who believe and trust God in the development of their children. You are still guiding me because you took time to introduce me to Christ, and that has made all the difference in my life.

The information shared in this book will benefit parents who choose to utilize these lessons learned from my parents. You will learn how to raise your children to be obedient to you, first. In turn, your children will transfer that obedience to God and learn to care about others more than they care about themselves.

Thank you, Mom and Dad, for being who you still are to me, and to the many others you fathered and mothered. I pray these lessons learned will help even those who did not have both parents realize that God is their father, and even without their earthly parents, He will teach them all things if they trust Him.

Lessons Learned

Model what you expect your child to live.

My parents did not do a lot of talking to us to teach us valuable lessons. They lived their lives in such a way that we "caught more than we were taught," so I learned the following by *watching* my parents.

Love your enemies as yourself.

I saw my mother "love the hell" right out of people. There were many times when I saw people mistreat my mom, but she would continue to smile earnestly and say what was important for her to say, in the spirit of meekness, and leave the results to God. I never saw her argue with anyone! However, after she left the conversation, there was silence in the room because her profound words, that had to come straight from the Holy Spirit, left the person speechless to retaliate.

I saw my mother treat one woman in particular with this type of love for years—I mean years—and one day, the woman came to my mother in tears and repented for all the years she mistreated my mom. She knew she would be forgiven. There was no doubt because for all those years, my mom never did anything but love her. I watched this scenario from preadolescence until my teenage years, and I remember talking to my mom on several occasions about what I personally wanted to do to let the lady know I did not appreciate the way she was treating my mom. My mom would always tell me, "This is a teachable moment baby. There is no need to retaliate. I don't take personally anything she does to me because I know I have not done anything to her to deserve the treatment. Remember, you catch more bees with honey than with vinegar." These were my mom's famous last words (smile), so one of my mantras has always been, **"Don't take it personally."** This has been very helpful in my life. Understanding this has helped me get along with people—no matter where they were coming from.

I will never forget when I was in the fourth grade, and I internalized this lesson in a way that was pretty profound for a ten year old, I would say. A boy in my class was sitting behind me pulling my hair. I kept asking him to stop, but he kept picking with me, either pulling my hair or pushing me very slightly on my shoulder. I moved my desk forward, hoping he could not reach me, but he also moved his forward. Finally, he said to me, "Your mama." I jumped out of my chair and hit him so hard he fell backward in his chair, and his feet kicked his desk over. Needless to say, we disrupted the entire class. Of course, the teacher came over, and I found myself in the front office. When my mom arrived and found out what happened, she made a statement that I have not forgotten to this day. She said, "Baby, you won the battle, but he won the war." Wow, there I was, ten years old, and I actually got it. She was saying, he doesn't even know your mama. He just knew that remark would get a reaction from you. If you had not taken that personally, you would still be in your classroom and not in the principal's office. I will never forget that lesson, so this has been one of my mantras ever since, "If you know you have not done anything to cause a person's negative treatment toward you, **don't take it personally**." My mom helped me understand the little boy probably just liked me and didn't know any other way to express it.

I learned empathy for people because of this situation. I felt so badly about embarrassing this boy after knocking him over in his seat that I actually apologized to him. After this incident, I became very intent on helping others. How I helped others became more important to me than getting something in return for my help. I realize now how important this lesson was because when you really understand the word "love," you know it is an action word. When you love someone with the love that only comes from God (agape love), you do not expect anything in return. Agape love is unconditional. It is not natural and can only be achieved through the Spirit within you. I learned this lesson early in life because of my parents' modeling of this action toward others and because they helped me exemplify this in my attitude and actions.

I have had people who did not even know me come to me and tell me things about their lives. At the time, I did not understand why people had chosen to share with me their personal situations. I realize now that the Spirit of God in me shines toward others, and people see something in me that makes them feel safe to share things. I do not take this lightly, and I have learned to minister to people from all walks of life when they give me the opportunity to do so. This is why **meeting people where they are** is very important. Sometimes, all a person needs is someone to listen. No words are necessary. I saw both of my parents masterfully practice this with others. As I grew older, I worked to incorporate this skill into my life.

I learned to love studying the Word of God by watching my dad, every single day of his *life, study the Word of God.*

I remember, every day, my dad would sit on the couch that sat directly under the bookcase that held part of his library, and he would read his Bible. Sometimes, he would stare in space, and I would ask him, "What are you thinking about

Dad?" And he would answer, "Just talking to my Lord." I heard this quite a bit because for some reason, even though I knew what the answer was going to be, I would still ask. Not only did I ask, so did my sisters.

I would sit on the couch next to my dad and read my Bible beside him. Sometimes, I would read other books, as well. When I had questions, he would let me interrupt him and ask whatever I needed to know. My mom taught my sisters and me to respect our dad's study time. Often, when I would sit next to him, I would write my questions down rather than ask him right away. Then, while we were eating dinner at the table, I would ask my questions. That was a lot of fun because the whole family got a chance to give input to my thoughts. I loved that time of fellowship.

I learned the Bible is the best book, but it's not the only book you should study.

My dad always told us, "Study the Bible, and know it well enough to have a solid belief in God that cannot be shaken by every wind or wave of religious talk that comes your way." He told us to make the Bible our first and most important book to understand. Then, read everything that others read to understand their stance in religious beliefs, so we would be prepared to witness to them by **meeting them where they are.**

Meeting people where they are is my second mantra. I studied Jesus thoroughly—how He reacted and responded to people in the Bible when He met them, how He ministered to them at their point of need, and how He used language they would understand based on who they were. He is the master of meeting people where they are. I was not smart enough to pursue this study of Him on my own; my dad encouraged me to do so. Three really great examples from Jesus that have always stood out to me are (1) the way He ministered to the woman at the well, (2) the way He used language the fishermen would under-stand, and (3) how He used the metaphor of harvesting grapes. He said, "I am the vine, ye are the branches" (John 15:5). Another episode in Jesus' life that stood out to me was when He was going to the cross. After explaining to His disciples that He was the Son of Man and word spread about who He was, He was asked several times to repeat His claim publicly. However, Jesus did not repeat himself because He knew they were going to persecute Him for saying He was the King. When the High Priest asked again, "You said you are the King?" He replied, "So you say." This exchange has always intrigued me because Jesus forced them to say what He knew was the truth. Sometimes, Jesus answers with a question to force people to think through what they are asking. There are also times when He does not give an answer at all for the same reason.

This type of analytical thinking came from my parents helping me to think through things. I have embodied this analytical attitude throughout my life, and I always read with a critical eye.

I learned that "head knowledge is not enough."

My mom and dad used this statement all the time. They were making sure we knew that studying the Word of God is not the only thing you have to do to ensure it becomes a part of you. *Knowing the Word* and *making it a part of your life* are two very distinct things. When I understood this lesson, it haunted me, in a way. It made me think twice about everything I did (smile).

This was one of the lessons that helped me manage peer pressure easily. There was a game my friends played while we were growing up called "Chicken." They would dare each other to stand on the line in the middle of the street while cars were rushing by. I never played the game and had no problem with them calling me "chicken" because I remembered something my mom told us at a very early age, "I'd rather be a live chicken, than a dead duck." Again, teachable moments at the dinner table stood out and taught me valuable lessons. I was never bothered with peer pressure, and I truly think it was because of the teachable moments at the dinner table.

I learned to love history.

My dad also studied historical books. He would actually read almanacs. He studied the history of lynching, and he studied Africa. He studied everything that fully told the story of who we are as African Americans, including who we are in Christ. I have that same strong desire to study our history, connecting our genealogical and our spiritual identities. I also love ministering to others to help them understand the same, but I know I am just the seed planter and not the one responsible for convincing the person. That is the work of the Holy Spirit, once the seed is planted. Thank God for that (smile).

I became an avid reader, just like my dad.

When my dad read the Bible, he always did further research. I would see him with several other study guides as he read to prepare his sermons. I acquired the same type of study habits. When I studied, I always dug deeper with my research. I never did just surface studying, so I usually received outstanding grades on reports and research papers.

A book mobile would come to our neighborhood in the summer. I won several book reading contests where in one single summer, I read 100 books. I absolutely loved reading. I traveled the world through reading. I learned about other cultures through reading. To this day, I love reading, especially the Word of God.

I learned to meditate on the Word after reading it. My dad always sat and meditated on the Word. We learned to recognize when he was meditating, and we would not interrupt him. When I began to meditate on the Word, I realized that God would actually speak understanding to you as you meditated. It became a great part of my quiet time with God that I cherished at a very young age.

I learned to be thorough in everything I did.

My mom used to take me to NAACP meetings, Ministers' Wives meetings, and Baptist conventions, and I would actually work alongside her to do her duties in whatever office she held. I remember working with her to produce the church bulletin each week. We had a mimeograph machine at the church, and I learned to use that machine and help her each week. I also learned to type at an early age, and in order for me not to get stuck typing with one finger on each hand, my mom bought me a typing book when I was only in fourth grade. She told me to learn the right fingering on the keys. The summer before my sixth-grade year in school, she sent me to summer school to take typing, and I remember being the only little child in the class with all adults. I came out of the class typing 40 wpm, higher than anyone else in the class. I think often about the wisdom in that decision. My mom typed with one finger on each hand and was very fast typing like that, but she did not want me to get stuck there. Typing is one of the skills I really excelled in, and now I type over 100 wpm easily. When I had children, I made sure they learned this skill, as well, because I knew the career advantage it would give them. Even though my boys resisted, they were thankful for this skill when they got older.

On another note, my parents always taught us that being on time is being 15 to 30 minutes early, at the latest. Our family was never late to any activity. You cannot get somewhere exactly at the time it starts and be ready to start working. You always have to get settled first, and that takes time. So, on time is getting there early.

Encourage your children and tell them you love them.

My mom always told us she loved us. Interestingly enough, we did not do a lot of hugging in our family. As I think about that, it seems strange. But the interactions we had with my parents were somewhat a hug. We heard the words "I love you" at least once a day. We knew they were not just words because the words always equaled outward actions that showed us we were loved. Throughout the day, just the things my mom did showed she loved us. She was not a mom who hollered and screamed at you. She always had a quiet, loving demeanor, even when she had to chastise you. In fact, my sisters and I have always said we would feel so badly when we did something wrong that we preferred she give us a spanking rather than talk to us. Her face was always the picture of love, even when you had done something wrong. She had a way of loving you in spite of yourself. It taught me to do the same for others.

My daughter honored my mom with a statement she said to her one day. She said, "You've always been a grandma, haven't you?" I knew exactly what she meant. A grandma just loves you all the time; Grandma is not the one who chastises you. Grandma spoils you. Grandma is a picture of love and a source of wisdom for a child. That was a very profound statement, and it made me think about the many grandparents who don't get a chance to fulfill this role alone. They have to play the role of mom and dad. I thank God for the wisdom my daughter had in honoring her grandmom, my mom, with these words.

Make all of your decisions based on God's Word. In other words, don't tell your children to do something "because I said so."

Always line your answers up with a statement that directly connects back to the character of God. When you lead and guide your children by absolute truth—you live it. You teach it by modeling it, and it is the best gift you can give your child.

I truly believe my parents were before their time, or maybe a better way to put it is, they were parents who followed the parental guide book (the Bible) during a time when others were still saying (and believing), "Children don't come with a guidebook." I remember also thinking there was no guidebook, but a few years ago, the light came on. The Bible is that guidebook. For instance, if my mom or dad caught us in a lie, they would tell us not to lie "because God is honest, and you want to be just like Him." Rather than say, *"Because I told you so,"* which is usually the canned answer for everything when we do not know how to answer, they would answer with the reason—which was straight from the Word of God. If I was mean and hateful to someone, rather than say, "Don't do that because I said so," my parents would say, "You should not mistreat others because God is love, and He would have you treat the person the way you want to be treated." Again, their guidance was directly from the Word of God, to love your neighbor as yourself. What an ingenious way to teach your children about the character-istics of a loving God. They brought everything back to absolute truth—God's Word. This approach was one of the most profound teachable moments because not only was I learning to be obedient to them, I was also learning the character of God and the importance of my obedience to Him.

Systematically instruct your child by having regular family devotions.

I knew my mom and dad were passionate about their relationship with God. I knew they truly loved God and trusted His Son Jesus with all their hearts. They showed it over and over as they trusted Him for things that could only be achieved by miracles. I saw them pray for things that seemed so farfetched, yet I saw their prayers answered over and over. They would include us in many of their prayers, and we would pray for people who were sick, our family members who were lost, our neighbors who were living unhealthy lifestyles, our schools, our community, the elected officials in the city, and even the president of the United States. Many times, I felt things were being orchestrated right from my home because when we prayed about important issues and things changed according to what we prayed for, in my mind, I truly believed it was because my family and I prayed together. We would also celebrate God answering our prayers, so I started praying for things very early in life and believing God was going to answer my prayers. This type of modeling demonstrates how teaching your children to take time to spend with God can shape their worldview.

I started to develop my personal time with God at a young age. I remember going off by myself and having long conversations with God, and actually receiving answers. I truly thought of Jesus as a friend because for as long as I could remember, my mom always talked about having Jesus as her friend. One of her favorite songs was "What a Friend We Have in Jesus," and I can hear her voice singing that song every time that song is sang in church. I remember the day when Jesus said to me that I was also His friend. This was a key moment in my life because I was only 12 years old. Although I knew He called me friend, I never said it to anyone, and I am still not sure why at that early age I had already felt it was something I should keep to myself. I could say He is *my* best friend, but I could not say He called me *His* friend.

I guess I thought I was unworthy to be called His friend (and of course, I am), but sharing this should not be hard to do. I am still growing in this area (smile).

Not only did I see my parents spend their personal time with God, but they also spent family time with us during the week. Our schedules were busy as a family, but they never neglected time with us. My mom or dad (or both) was present at every play or sports event that we participated in while growing up, and family dinner served as time for teachable moments, as we would discuss the school day and other situations in our lives. With three girls in the family, there was always something new to talk about.

Make sure your answers to your children's questions come straight from the Word of God, the Holy Bible.

My parents taught me that God's Word has an answer for everything! There is nothing the Word of God does not deal with—nothing!

Although I remember only getting one spanking in my entire life, it was the love with which we were chastised that made me feel so badly about the reprimands. It was as if I had received a spanking with a belt. I did not want to displease my parents. As parents, this is exactly where we want our children to get because these feelings of remorse for sin will lead to repentance and godly sorrow. It is not until we are godly sorrowful for a sin committed—when it hurts us to hurt God—

that we come to a point of experiencing a true, loving relationship with God.

Married couples should always have a united front when disciplining their children so the children will not feel they can divide and conquer.

I learned this by experiencing the opposite happen in my own marriage. Once I reflected on the way my mom and dad handled things, it stimulated some very productive conversations between my husband and me. I never remember seeing my parents argue, but it was obvious they had discussed certain things and had come to a decision about situations that pertained to us girls. They could not be separated and manipulated by us at all, and I know they had to differ in their opinions on discipline because their personalities were very different. However, they did a masterful job of staying united when it came to disciplining their daughters.

When children learn to divide and conquer at home, it gives them a false sense they can manipulate situations everywhere, and they find themselves in precarious situations outside of the home. I speak from personal experience, as my husband and I had to correct our own children after we made the mistake of not being on one accord. Thank God for grace and mercy!

Daughters will learn how to be treated by men by watching how their dad treats their mom.

My dad loved my mother very much. I can remember one time when he thought someone at church had done something improper to my mom. He sure took care of that (smile)! It was that day that I understood why my mom took care of things herself and did not tell my dad about every little thing that someone at church had said or did to her. As the pastor of a church, his hands were full. Though my dad was a man of God, when he was angry, he reminded me of the time when Jesus found the men turning the house of God into a "den of thieves." There was this look that my dad would get on his face that let you know he was displeased. Then, he would catch the look and turn it into a smile, but the words he spoke really went with a frown. It was really funny. He did very well not allowing the anger to lead him to sin, but I knew he had to work on it. In our family, we call it your "face talking." I picked this up from my dad, as well. One time, my mom said to me, "Barbara, you might as well tell them to go to hell because your face is saying it anyway." That was a true wake-up call for me. I have worked on my "face talking" ever since. Though it still does sometimes (smile).

My parents did a great job of creating the balance we needed as pastor's children. They allowed us to grow up as regular children, participating in sports, going to school socials, and other things. My dad was the first person to teach me how to dance. It was in our home that Dad taught my sisters and me the two-step. He was such a well-rounded man. He was a semi-professional base-ball player growing up and was the pitcher on his team, and my mom was a great basketball player in high school (she never told us this until we learned it at a family reunion). My sisters and I were also very athletic. My dad would take us outside, play catch with us, race with us. We really enjoyed his time with us.

My parents taught us the ways of God and then allowed us to put them to work in our daily lives. There was another family of children in our small city whose father was also a pastor. They were forced to wear long dresses, and they could not attend football and basketball games, and especially not socials at school. I recognized how important a sacrifice my parents were making for us. Although I am sure they worried about us sometimes, they trusted God to keep us. They gave us opportunities to learn lessons while we were home with them, and we had the cushion to make some mistakes. Since we were there with them, they could correct us when needed. This was very important in our lives.

Sons will learn how to understand certain things about women from their mom.

Although we did not have brothers, my mom had a sister who died at 33 years old, and her only son was like a brother to us. He would come to stay with us often. I would hear my mom talking to him about how to respond to girls. She made some very profound statements to him. One that stands out to me is, *"Men and women are different. What a woman says and what a man hears are two different things, and vice versa. You have to be sensitive to girls and have their best at heart."* I will never forget that. She was telling my cousin, when he was 16 years old, to protect the girls from themselves when he knew they were attracted to him. A young woman often gets involved with her heart when a young man may not at the moment.

That was very wise of my mother to say. If we had more young men who thought this way, premarital sex would not be such a big problem because both sexes would take on purity as their personal responsibility.

Making the Grade

These last two lessons are dear to me. There is something very significant about the relationship between girls and their dads and sons and their mothers and what girls and boys learn from these parent-child relationships about how to interact with the opposite sex. A lot of the information I work very hard to share with young people came directly from the things I learned from my parents. The best thing they could have taught me was to have a personal relationship with Christ. There are some things that only God can teach you because He is the only One who knows all about you.

My parents did a great job of being stewards over us and making sure we understood that our obedience to them would one day transfer into obedience to God. If we did not learn to be obedient to them, we were going to have a hard time being obedient to God.

You would think with all of this great teaching we would be the perfect children. Of course, that was not the case (smile), but I know I was better because of my parents' teachings. I still made mistakes, but I did not waddle in them. I got up quickly and had a spirit of repentance. Because I had learned early in life to love God for myself, I did not want to hurt Him.

My parents let us know they were not perfect, but their goal was always to strive to be like Jesus. By implementing these parental lessons, you will teach your children to

- **Make wise decisions** (Philippians 19:11)
- **Learn to keep their commitments** (Proverbs: 20:6)
- **Care genuinely about others, and realize early on that "it's simply not about them"** (John 15)

When obedience is achieved and your child transfers his or her primary love from dependence on you to dependence on and love for Jesus Christ, then you can say you received an "A" as a parent through the grace and power of God.

ABOUT THE AUTHOR

Barbara Spencer Dunn and her husband of 43 years, Carl M. Dunn, reside in Prince George's County, Maryland. They have three children: Carlvern Maurice Dunn (Paula (Graham) Dunn), Byron Antonio Dunn, and Rhonda Rochelle Evans. Mrs. Dunn grew up and attended public schools in Amarillo, Texas during the height of the Civil Rights Movement. She is a graduate of Bowie State University and has also studied at Maple Springs Baptist Church Bible College and Seminary, with a focus on Christian counseling. She is the recipient of several community service awards for her extensive work in communities around the country. Mrs. Dunn's presentations educate people of all cultures, blend generational divides, enlighten youth, reengage the church community, and cause intellectuals to refocus their thinking in a way that reflects Dr. Carter G. Woodson's goals in his seminal work, *The Mis-Education of the Negro* (1933).

Dunn co-authored *Training with a Purpose* (2010) with her son Carlvern, and she is also the author of *Before and Beyond the Niagara Movement: As the Youth See It* (2011). She seeks to provide tools that promote the unification of mankind. The release of *Lessons Learned from My Parents* is her gift to younger generations in hopes of continuing the parental wisdom of the elder generations.

Made in the USA
Charleston, SC
17 June 2012